ALSO BY THE AUTHORS

SNAPS

DOUBLE SNAPS

TRIPLE SNAPS

YOU'RE SO FINE,
I'D DRINK A TUB OF YOUR BATHWATER

YOU'RE SO *fine,*

I'D DRINK A TUB OF YOUR BATHWATER

over 500 no-fail pickup lines that work on the bus, in the bar, in the neighborhood store

STEPHAN DWECK & MONTERIA IVEY INTRODUCTION BY VERONICA WEBB

HYPERION
NEW YORK

Library of Congress Cataloging-in-Publication Data

Dweck, Stephan.
You're so fine, I'd drink a tub of your bathwater : (over 500 no-fail pickup lines that work on the bus, in the bar, in the neighborhood store) / by Stephan Dweck and Monteria Ivey.
p. cm.
ISBN 0-7868-8202-6
1. Afro-American wit and humor. 2. Man-woman relationships—Humor. 3. Interpersonal communication—Humor. 4. Dating (Social customs)—Humor. 5. Black English. 6. Americanisms. I. Ivey, Monteria. II.Title.
PN6231.N5D94 1997
818'.5402—dc20   96–20116
                                                              CIP

Designed by Jill Gogal

First Edition

10   9   8   7   6   5   4   3   2   1

To Lisa Jones, Kellie Jones, Maria Perez, and Stephanie Jones, and all the Divas who can laugh at a good pickup line.

—L. Stephan Dweck

To the "Douglas Crew," who taught me, when it comes to women, it's not always what you say, but how you say it that counts.

—Monteria Ivey

Table of Contents

Thanks to our editor, Leslie Wells
Whose energy, enthusiasm, and sincerity inspired us
to dig deep into our creative well.

Special thanks
To our agents Barbara Lowenstein and Nancy K. Yost,
and all the talented people at Hyperion.

We appreciate the support of these people
James Percelay, Donna Campbell, Yalda Teheranian,
Dedra Tate, Jerome Leventhal, Jim Grant, Veronica
Webb, Dr. Geneva Smitherman, Dr. Gloria Randle, Cooper
Cunningham, Kendall Minter, Linda Burke, Claude Ismael,
Tina Douglass, Carole Green, Debbie Pender, Michelle
Green, Jeanine DuBison, Yvette Coit, Persina Lucas,
Mercedes Ayala, Valerie Legg, Larry Dais, Arlene Levine,
Gary Sharfin, Michael Lewittes, Sharon Alexander,
Matthew Jordan Smith, Jason Spitz, Sandy Epstein,
Howard and Karen Baldwin, Steven Slotnick, Jeff
Gordon, Cary Granat, David Colden, Channing Johnson,
Bob Weinstein, Irene Dreyer, and Suzanne DePasse.

Thanks to our research assistants,
Michelle Cuccuini, Chester Mapp

Introduction

Why do relationships occupy so much of our thinking? Because if they didn't, we would be extinct. Think about it. Isn't everything ultimately about sex and pleasure? That's why we go to work. That's why we study. That's why we get dressed up. It's all part of the *mating dance*, and everything we do is designed to help us end up in the dance. When it's time for romance people are the same all over the world. The common bond is that men love to chase, and women love being chased. Think of it as a primal desire. That's why kids play tag. We all secretly fantasize about being taken as a prisoner (of love).

Here's where the right line comes into play. The chase has to be right. The man better come with his shit correct. Imagine one of those wild animal kingdom shows on television. Sometimes the predator (man) can be overzealous, only to be immediately outsmarted by the prey (woman).

Coming correct means you have got to have *style*. And style means a unique and pleasingly attractive way of putting lines together. Black men have the most style, no question. I think the reason can be found within the culture. Having a developed sense of linguistics is a status symbol, like having a Lexus, or a pair of hundred-dollar sneakers, or wavy hair.

Women have to be on the lookout for men who try to use material things as compensation for weak lines. How much material items can compensate varies from woman to woman. Personally, I'm very language oriented, so if you're really not interesting to talk to, then I can't be interested in you. Some women like material things, and the guy with more money is in a position to make bigger promises. This can be attractive, until you get some experience. Then you learn whenever a man starts promising you something, girl . . . run!

Now if a woman is making money, it can

change your whole criteria. It's not that you don't have the same feelings, but you do have different expectations. A guy wearing an expensive suit might be able to get over with a line that a brother wearing jeans wouldn't dare drop. Unless the brother in the jeans is really, really fine. Always remember, guys, fine can make us overlook a lot, but fine cannot override "corny."

I think the one place where you are most likely to hear corny lines is right out on the street. When I hear some really lame line, my first thought is usually, "Why am I being harassed and insulted?" Then I think, "This guy must be crazy, and I know better than to fuck with crazy people, so let me just keep on walk-

4

ing." Some situations on the street can be really frightening, especially when you're alone and there are a group of guys. When there's a group, guys get bold. It turns into a power thing, because some guy wants retribution for every time he was ever turned down by a woman. They know you're defenseless. What am I going to do, turn around and knock him out?

This is why women go out expecting to be bombarded with lines. It doesn't matter if you're out for the evening or just walking down the street. We get tired of hearing ". . . ooh baby, I like what you got under that skirt . . ." or being followed because of what we're wearing.

Women have to plan their whole day, every

day, dressing for safety. Guys are always on the prowl, but women are not always looking to be preyed upon. It's like the game is going on, whether you like it or not. That's the part that's not fun.

The element of surprise is what makes the setting unique for a pickup line. I remember one incident that occurred in a dressing room. I was in there with a guy, a hairdresser, whom I'd known for a year. Suddenly it struck me that he was looking at me. "What are you looking at?" "It's just that you have so much body, and you look so good to me." Now I'm looking at him and I'm thinking, ". . . so much body? Hello? I'm a 34A. Are you crazy?" (For all you guys who don't know, that's the smallest bra there is, next to a training bra.) I just looked at him and said, "Oh my God. All this time, and you were just perpetrating as a homosexual!"

The lines in this book are timeless. They'll always be around, because there's always a need for a good line. Some of the lines are different today because of the influence of hip-hop. Sometimes guys on the street try to get my attention by calling me "caramel sunbeam."

I don't think anything will take the place of lines being passed down from one generation to the next; and as long as that's true, women will keep on giving advice to each other so they can stay ready. We tell each other things like,

"Girl, don't let him dog you . . . Keep his pants up and your skirt down . . . Get some rent in your pocket before you get some dick in your drawers . . . Girl, when you go out, start selecting and rejecting."

One of the chapters in this book deals with what women would like to hear from men. The first thing you guys need to know is that women understand that what you say and what you do are two totally different things. Men just need to know, don't lie. Put some sincerity behind those lines.

But assuming there are some good men out there, just remember that once you get the woman, change the lines to compliments.

Remind her that, "Yes, you are groovy and good-looking, and the apple of my eye."

—Veronica Webb

A Few Words from the Authors

When we first sat down to discuss what this book was going to be about, we had a simple idea. "Let's write about the one subject that occupies the greatest amount of time in the lives of just about everyone—relationships." It seems as if we're always just getting into or trying to get out of or wondering when will I be or wishing I had never been . . . in a relationship. With that settled, the trick was to find a new spin on a favorite topic.

I was awakened early one morning by a familiar voice on my answering machine.

"I know you're there. Roll over and pick up the phone." It was Stephan. "I got it! What's the hardest part about meeting someone new?"

"I don't know. I guess . . . figuring out how to start the conversation. You've got to step correct."

"You know it. The right line could mean the difference between getting a phone number or a cold shoulder."

The genesis for a new book was created.

It would have been too easy to go to guys and ask them for their best pickup lines. What guy would be willing to admit that his favorite line

is actually . . . corny. We decided it would be better to go to the people who have to listen to (and
put up with) these lines to find and separate the
best from the worst. We interviewed women
from across the country, from various age
groups, and different walks of life.

We don't want the guys to think that we're
completely biased. A handful of gentlemen from
across the country were selected to participate in
our search. We focused on men who have a
great deal of contact with the public, and this
allowed them to give their lines with the dis-
claimer that these were pickups "that I've heard
other guys use."

We learned a few things along the way

(which is why we included a chapter on lines women would like to hear). Whether we were talking over drinks in New York's Greenwich Village, or sitting on a porch in North Carolina, or hanging out in the windy city of Chicago (on a night when the infamous "hawk" was definitely out), we found that women have some universal feelings about men. When it comes to communicating, the general consensus was that women say what they feel while men say one thing, but mean something else.

Carried over to pickup lines, it seems that a lot of guys simply don't have a clue. What we see as smooth and sophisticated often comes across as tired and corny. In fact, that's why we included some "comeback" lines from the women. There's no quicker way to deflate the male ego than to counterpunch a weak line.

Trust us, men, we're on your side. So for all of you who might need a little help (and who among us couldn't use an assist every now and then), here are over 500 of the best tried and proven lines for your personal use. As a bonus, we've even included some "flat" lines that you should be sure to avoid if you want to make the best possible impression. As for the ladies, we believe you'll enjoy seeing in print all the lines that made you laugh, cringe, and sometimes smile. Enjoy!

—Stephan Dweck and Monteria Ivey

Baby, I'll give you a tongue bath no germ could live through.

I don't want to be your boyfriend, I just want to give him a little help.

That's a nice dress. It would look great crumpled up at the foot of my bed.

If you let me in your enchanted forest, I'll let you play with my magic wand.

It must be your birthday, 'cause you have a hell of a cake back there.
Comeback: Well . . . you'll never blow out these candles!

Hi, my name is Frank. Don't forget it, because you'll be screaming it later tonight.

Is it true that black blondes have more fun?

Would you like gin and platonic, or do you prefer scotch and sofa?

If I give you my number, what are the odds that you will use it?
Comeback: Slim and none.

If I die, I want to come back as those jeans and wear your ass out.

What will it take for me to become your friend?

I'm not looking for "Miss Right," I'm looking for "Miss Right Now."

You look so good, I would support you and your husband.

Sexy, I know your man is a hunchback, a dwarf, and a cripple, so treat yourself to a real man.
Comeback: That's okay, I'll continue to date the handicapped.

I went to my urologist and he told me that I need to have sex at least twice a week, so I don't get backed up. Can you help a brother out?
Comeback: No, but I do have a plunger.

So, what do you do for a living?
Comeback: Female impersonator.

Hi, I just moved to the city and was wondering if you could recommend a restaurant?

Comeback: Sure, there's a restaurant called Eat Alone down the block.

I know you know who my ex is, but actually all the time I was with her, I wanted to be with you.

Girl, you're so fine, if my eyes were teeth, they would fall out black and rotten just looking at you.

Sweetheart, stick your finger in my tea and make it sweet.

Good gracious alive! You got all the ass and no hips.

Baby, you must be tired, because you've been running through my mind all day.

23

All that sweetness and I'm a diabetic.

Baby, you look as happy as a Mormon getting a lap dance.

Oh baby, I'd love to be your genie and grant you three wishes.
Comeback: Okay. First, I'd wish you would stop talking. Second, I'd wish you would turn around. Third, I'd wish you'd disappear.

What's a girl like you doing in a place like this?
Comeback: Trying to avoid men like you who use lines like that.

Baby, I'm not this tall, I'm just sitting on my wallet.

Can I end this sentence with a proposition?

Baby, if this bar is a meat market, you must be prime rib.

Damn, love, I'd do anything to be that piece of gum in your mouth.

If you leave my sight right now, I'll drop dead.
Comeback: Is that a promise?

Baby, all those curves and me with no brakes.

Hey baby, you need some salt with that shaker?

You know I've been watching you not watching me.

Excuse me, does your boyfriend have what I have?
Comeback: Yes, but he went to the doctor to get penicillin.

Baby, you're so fine, I'd never cheat on you . . . well uh, maybe just once.

Sexy, don't judge me by my looks, judge me by my reputation. I'm a good dog.

Hi! Am I too short for your affection?

Baby, for me, freedom means being your slave.

Sweetheart, you're so fine. If your face was on money, I wouldn't spend a goddamn dime.

Do you believe in love at first sight? Or do I have to walk by again?

If you got a minute, I could be yours for a lifetime.

Hi, it's an open bar—can I buy you a drink?

Your name must be honey, 'cause you look naturally sweet.

I'm having so many problems with my girl, I think
you would be the perfect other woman.

You're so fine, I'll give you the key to my house,
my car, and my heart. Just don't lose them.

Are you here alone, or is the big guy coming this
way your brother?

Excuse me, I seem to have lost my phone number.
Can I borrow yours?

I just saw my psychic, and he told me you should go out with me.

I can't stay, my Porsche is double-parked. Can I have your phone number?

Damn baby, can I get an application to take you out?

Girl, you look so good, if I was your husband, I'd be too afraid to allow you out the house.

Do you have a man? Yes? How long have you had that problem?

Baby, you're so fine, you got me worried. But first thing tomorrow morning, I'm filing for divorce.

Excuse me, do you have peanuts in your pants, 'cause I would love to taste them.

I know I'm a dog, but can I get a second interview?

Hi, if you're waiting to exhale, I have a Breathalyzer.

I really thought you would be snotty, but instead you're beautiful and snotty.

Would you like someone to mix with your drink?

Do you mind if I stare close, instead of across the room?

I'm new in town, could you give me directions to your apartment?

Are you cold? You should be, you've been naked in my mind all night.

Baby, you're so fine, I wouldn't even use a condom with you.
Comeback: Well, I would have to use a mask with you.

Can I have your number? . . . No? Okay, then your neighbor's number?

Can I blow in your ear? I really do have nice breath.

Your lips are so sweet, they make candy jealous.

Could you move your hair? I would love to blow on your neck.

If you're looking for Mr. Right, I'm here.

Could I have your autograph?

I know you probably wouldn't, but would you take the phone number of a stranger?
Comeback: You're right, I wouldn't.

Sweetheart, you've got more moves than Jell-O, and there is always room for Jell-O.

Here's my card, can we go out to dinner?

Hi, didn't you give me your number earlier? Could I have it one more time?

Pardon me, baby, can I have your permission to dream about you tonight?

Baby, just hearing your voice sends chills of anticipation tingling down my spine.

Oh! You look like a woman in love, but I'm here to give you more love.

Baby, you look so good, every time I hear a love song, I will think of you.

Honey, you're so sweet, I bet you shit sugar.

Hey baby, you down with the movement? 'Cause I would love to be your liberator.

Baby, you're so good-looking that if you are not here with your man, something must be wrong.

Sexy, if your flight's booked, can I get on standby?

Baby, you're all the woman I need, and I need a lotta' woman.

Hey baby, if you want quality time, I'm quality and I got time.

Do you come here a lot?
Comeback: No, but it sure looks like you do.

Excuse me, we haven't met, but I'm your future husband.

You're so fine you need a bodyguard to walk with you.

Tell me if your man is doing wrong, 'cause I'll do you right.

Why you got all the meat, and I'm sittin' over here eatin' bones?

Your husband is one lucky man. Is he here?

Oh baby, you're the person that I'm looking for.
Comeback: Why? I'm not a parole officer.

Baby, I'm not going to stop talking until I can take you home.

My wife doesn't understand me.
Comeback: If you weren't in a bar trying to pick me up, she would.

Oh baby, did you come out of *Vogue* magazine?
Comeback: If I did, I wouldn't be talking to you.

Baby, I wish I was your boss, so I could try to take advantage of you.

If you give me five minutes of your time, I'll make you mine.

Can I have your autograph, and phone number along with it?

Can I lick your tattoo?

Is your personality as pretty as your eyes?

Can I marry you now, or do I have to wait?

Baby, if you play your cards right, I'll take you home.

Hey girl, if you talk to me, I might tell you something you want to hear.

You look too good to be alone.

If you come home with me, I'll keep a smile on your face.

Can I be the father to your son?

Oh baby, I wish I knew the combination to that lock.

You should be arrested for looking so good.

Hey baby, I don't usually talk to anyone, but I'll break that rule for you.

Your man trust you alone?

I'll be the best man you ever met.

Baby, can I be your night watchman?

Baby, you deserve me.
Comeback: Why, have I sinned?

Hi, I look familiar. What's your name?

Hi, I'm single, desperate, and have no morals, but I'm open to being rehabilitated.

What's up, baby? Let me be your suntan superman.

This is a pretty place, but I haven't seen anything as splendid as you sitting there.

The voices in my head said that you should go out with me.

Excuse me, but I must tell you that your beauty is unfair to all the other women in the room.

Excuse me, what is your nationality?
Comeback: Leper.

You look shy, so I'll do the talking.

Can we talk about how beautiful you are?

Wouldn't you like to give me a ride in your car?
Comeback: Why? Can't get back to the zoo on your own?

Hey, didn't I see you at a party last week?
Comeback: No, it was a lineup.

Say, wasn't I married to you once?

This is your lucky day, 'cause I just happen to be single.
Comeback: I never was that lucky.

I've had a lot to drink, and you're beginning to look pretty good.

I thought women like you traveled in packs.

A skirt like you would make a man like me leave his happy home.

Just one touch, baby, your beauty is killing me.

I'd rather go blind than to see you walk away from me.

Do you appreciate a man who can cook? Because I would love to burn you up.

If looks were money, you would be rich.

Oh sexy, I wish I was your lipstick.

If I wasn't such a good man, I'd divorce my wife and marry you.

Oh, you have a boyfriend? Well, that's okay, we can still go out 'cause I got a girl.

Baby, you look so sweet, I'm gonna take you and buy you your own candy store.

Your man let you out looking that good?

country
LINES

Girl, I'd suck you like a piece of watermelon rind and lick you like a Tootsie Roll.

Oh girl, look at that chest. I want some gravy with that stuffing.

Baby, I heard that milk does the body good, but you must have ate the whole damn cow.

Baby, you're so fine that all the other women in the bar look like pigs in slop compared to you.

You're so fine, I could sop you up with a biscuit.

Hey girl, looks don't matter. I'll just wrap you in a flag and hump you for glory.

You're so fine, you're like a freshly baked pork chop.

Yum, yum! All that juicy beef and no napkins.

I'm so hungry, girl, you smellin' like a snack.

Baby, you look so good, I could chew you up like a piece of Juicy Fruit.

Girl, you're so fine, you make a grown man cry, weep, and wail.

51

Sweetheart, I know I'm in love, 'cause I'm looking at cornbread, greens, yams, and pork chops.

I loves you, like a fish loves water.

Don't lose a pound, I'll take all the buns and the butter.

Oh, baby! I may not have fish in my freezer, but I'd make room for that rump roast.

You're so sweet-looking, I'm getting cavities just looking at you.

52

You're as good-looking as a pig knuckle on Groundhog Day.

Baby, I don't need no dinner, I'll just munch on your bones.

You look as good as a pork bun sandwich.

Girl, if you was a baker, I would love to taste your buns.

Baby, you look so good, I'd bite you all over with a serpent's tooth until you gave me your number.

Is your father related to chitterlings, 'cause you the shit, girl!

How can I get next to you? Do I have to go out with your mama first?

Thinking of you makes my teeth hurt, you just too sweet.

You're so fine, I'd bite the head off a rattlesnake for you.

You look so good, I'll buy your clothes.

Woman, if your mama is this fine, I'll marry her, too!

54

Oh girl, you rough! Rougher than number nine sandpaper.

Damn, girl, you look finger-lickin' good.

Oh baby! Shake, bake, and fry with your bad self.

Girl, is you sweet potato or candied yams?

Baby, if I can't have the whole pie, I just want a slice.

Happy Mother's Day— you fly mama.

Baby, I'd seduce you like a snake in the garden of Eden.

You sure are short. It'll be easy for a man to make good loving to you.

Gorgeous, you and me together are like dogs and fire hydrants.

You look like cooked food out of my grandma's country kitchen, and I love my grandma's cooking.

The better the batter the better the butter!

Baby, you look so fine, you make me feel like a termite in a furniture factory.

You're so fine, you'd give a blind man sight.

Baby, you're all that with a bowl of biscuits.

Oh, baby! I got my saddle and I would love to ride you into the sunset.

Oh, baby! You've got lips, hips, and sweet fingertips.

Oh, baby, all that meat! Ain't nothing better than a big girl.

Girl, if you cook the way you walk, I'll eat the pot.

Baby, you look so good, you knock the taste out of my mouth.

Oh, baby, your breath is so sweet, it's like honey on toast that's between your toes.

bedroom LINES

As long as I have a face, you'll always have a place to sit.

Let's have a party and invite your pants to come down.

Hey girl, why don't you sit on my lap and we can talk about the first thing that pops up.

Tomorrow morning, do you want me to call you or nudge you?

That shirt is becoming on you. Of course, if I were that shirt, I would be coming on you, too.

Oh! You are my favorite flavor. Lucky you're not ice cream or you'd be all over my face by now.

Girl, I'll eat you like a piece of hot corn bread.

Hey girl, I'm the peanut butter, and I would love for you to spread me all over your bread.

Is that a mirror in your pocket? Because I can see myself in your pants.

Can I take you out to eat, or do you want me to eat you out?

Do you like computers, 'cause you're making my software hard.

Hi, I'm a pretty boy with a big stick.

Girl, I'm like Domino's pizza . . . if you don't come in 30 minutes, the next one is free.

64

When I look at you, all I want to do is go down-town and eat a little take-out.

Let's go to my place and do the things I'll tell everyone we did anyway.

The word of the day is legs. Let's go back to my place and spread the word!

My face is leaving in 15 minutes. Be on it!

Damn! I would love to be your dessert.

They say size doesn't matter. But after tonight, it will!

Anything drugs can do, I can do with my tongue.

Do you like jewelry? 'Cause I'd love to take you home and show you my big gem.

Hi, I'm taking a survey. Do you spit or swallow?

Do you have a match?
Comeback: Yes, your face and my ass.

Why don't we cut out all the B.S. and just get naked.

Do you sleep on your stomach? No? Can I?

How do you like your coffee in the morning? 'Cause I know you're gonna stay over.

Excuse me, are you a virgin?

We could make beautiful babies together; how about it?

Why you eating that chicken, when you could be eating me?

68

I would love to wrap you up, take you home, and eat you for dessert.

Baby, I know you got a man, but can I be your lap-dog?

Girl, with hors d'oeuvres like that, I can't wait to taste the entrée.

You're so fine, I'd give your daddy a blow job for having you.

Damn, girl, you look so good I could eat you for dinner.

You have nice legs. I wish you could wrap them around my face till my lungs turn black and blue.

Hey girl! I love it, but not in public. I like it in bed.

Hi. I never mix business and pleasure, but I would work overtime to get a look at your buns.

Chocolate ice cream is my favorite flavor. Can I lick you?

Oh girl, I love short women, because they say good screws come in small packages.

I love that dress, but you know what would really look good on you? Me!

Have you ever been licked until tears rolled from your eyes?

See this bulge? This bulge's for you.

You look sweeter than a candy stripe and I would love to lick the stripes off you.

You have bedroom eyes, so I know you must be good in the sack.

Do you know where you want to be tonight? I think you want to be at my place.

72

Excuse me, you dropped this back there. Where? My bedroom.

You don't need to look for love in all the wrong places, just my place.

Excuse me, miss, is that dress felt? Would you like it to be?

Oh baby, if I was an M&M, I would want to melt in your mouth and not in your hand.

Girlfriend, you look so hot, if my underwear was plastic, it would melt all over this bar.

I miss my teddy bear; would you sleep with me?

I like every muscle in your body, especially mine.

Baby, if you were a buffet, I'd lay you out on a table and take what I wanted.

Haven't we met before?
Comeback: Yes, I'm the receptionist at the V.D. clinic.

Nice dress. Can I talk you out of it?

Are those fuck me eyes or fuck you eyes?
Comeback: Neither, they're fuck off eyes!

Excuse me, don't you recognize me with clothes on?

Hi, I work as a beef inspector. Let's go to your place for an inspection.

Baby, what's your favorite position on extramarital sex?

There are just two things I'd say to you: good night and good morning.

I would die happy if I saw you naked just once.

Comeback: I would die, too!

I had a wet dream about you last night. Would you mind if I asked you to help clean it up?

If you lost your virginity, can I have the box it came in?

Be unique and different and say yes, that you will come home with me.

Baby, you sure look good, but can you mop and glow?

Baby, let's put our crotches together and swap gravy.

I bet I could guess your weight if you sat on my face.

You know, I'd fuck you so hard you'd learn from it.

Baby, you're so fine, I would use your G-string to floss with.

Hey baby, I haven't seen you in a while. You sure look different without my dick in your mouth.

Do you have a boyfriend? Well, when you want a man friend, come and see me.

Let's play cannonball. I'll lay down so you can blow the hell out of me.

Let's make like a couple of ghosts and wear some sheets out!

I'll put my pole in your hole and make you holler soul!

Oh, look at those feet! I'll bet your toes are clean enough to suck.

Why don't I have my people call your people and we'll get together and make our own people.

Hey girl, I'm thinking about laying a pipeline . . . you interested?

Baby, I'd lick you from head to toe, and fill your pockets with whatever you need.

You need someone to work that round butt of yours.

Your lips are so juicy and sweet, I'd have to suck them like a lemon.

If you were my chocolate bar, I would eat the chocolate first, then I would go after the nuts.

If I was black, would you wear me?

I wish I was your wash-cloth, so I could be all over your body.

I love that lollipop in your mouth. Can I take its place?

Are you going to give me your number, or am I going to have to stalk you?

I know we can make it, baby, because you're the rice and I'm the beans.

You have the most beautiful eyes; they're the color of Pepsi Cola.

Excuse me, have you ever been a man?

Are those real?

Wow, girl! You got a waist like a wasp and an ass like a horse.

Oh baby! Oh baby! I want to marry you, I want to marry you. When? February 31st.

I like your bracelets. Do they deflect bullets?

Girl, I'm on you like white on rice and black on Wesley Snipes.

Is that your hair or a weave?

Baby, I wish I was an astronaut, so I could land on that moon.

You look like you'd be into S&M. I know because I'm a medium.
Comeback: Oh really? You look like a small to me.

Your eyes are as blue as my toilet water.

86

A lot of women get an operation to enlarge their breasts, but girl you're naturally gifted.

I love a woman with hair on her legs.
Comeback: Then maybe you should date a chimp.

You're hope, I'm less, without you I'm hopeless.

That's a nice butt, can I have a ride?

Hey, didn't you eat dinner with me last night?

Oh girl! You look so good. I never saw you look good before.

Hi, could you marry me during lunch?

Hi, are you an actress, model, singer, dancer, or contortionist?

Girl, you got the body of life, the face of heaven, and one hell of an ass.

Girl, you're so fine, if you were Jell-O, the company would be sold out.

You're so fine, you could send a dog to reform school.

You're so fine, you're disgusting.

Hi. I can tell that you love pets. Would you help me bathe my dog?

Comeback: Why don't you just take a shower?

Hey baby, why don't you give me your number, so that you can make me lunch.

No shit. This is a compliment: you look like Big Bird.

Girl, you're so fine, I'd suck a fart out your ass.

I've got the ship, you got the harbor, let's tie it up for the night.

Girl, if you married me, you could be my domestic goddess.

If I was a bee, I'd sting the hell out of you.

I'm on house arrest, but when I get free I'm coming for the woman I want.

I found out my wife is gay, are you?

Hi, I'm wearing dinosaur underwear.

Your eyes are the same color as my hamster.

You sure don't sweat much for a fat chick.

You better help me across the street, girl, 'cause your beauty just blinded me.

You look so good, you make me want to kiss your father.

I'm thirsty, save me a cup of bathwater.

A mind is a terrible thing to waste, but I wouldn't waste your booty.

Girl, you can float my boat.

You're so fine, I know you're the mother of my kids.

You look like you got money, and I'm Chemical . . . make a deposit.

I got to take you out, 'cause your ass is pumping like a Reebok.

Girlfriend, I would love to get in your pants.
Comeback: Why? I already have one asshole.

Don't I know you? Weren't you in my class on chilling at the Y?

If you want to get with a winner, you need to drop that man that you call a chicken dinner.

Girl, you're so fine, you should be gang married.

I don't need a beeper on my hip, all I need is your number on my lips.

How you doing, chocolate? You remind me of a Hershey Bar. Good enough to eat.

Hey love, can I get those seven digits?

Your boots are nice and I would love to knock them.

Everytime I look at your onion, it brings tears to my eyes.

Sexy, you going to hit me off or what?!

Yo shorty, what's the verdict? Is it you and me, or are you settin' me free?

So what's up! My body's banging like a Benz, and I want to get with you.

Honey, let go of that zero, and get with this hero.

Yo baby, when you gonna scratch me with those nails?

Damn, girl, your caramel complexion smells like cinnamon.

Yo, my wife is pregnant. It would be nice to feel a flat stomach. Can I feel yours?

As long as we together, yo, that's how we'll flow.

Do fries go with that shake?

Oh girl, gimme some of that!

Is your father a terrorist? Because you're the bomb.

I got a Jeep outside, and I would love to climb those mountains.

You are the squirrel in my world and I'm just try-ing to get a nut.

Yo! Dredlock sista, what's up with those digits?

Do you have a job, 'cause I want you to be my baby's mother.

Oh girl, how can I be down with your black-ness?

Yo baby! You packing mad goods.

Baby, you should go into boxing, 'cause you're a knockout.

Oh girl, you look strapped down. I would need to take caution with you.

If you'll be my superwoman, I'll be your superman and together we can fly.

Word up baby, you all I need.

Yo baby, I've seen girls who was dime pieces, but you a gold mine.

Monique, Monique . . . with the nice physique.

Suky, suky baby, I wish I was your sugar daddy.

You remind me of my Jeep. I want to wax it and it's easy to ride.

Baby, you got it going on, and then some.

Hey, brown eyes and caramel skin, can I talk to you?

Can I scoop you like ice cream?

Can I get to know you butter?

Baby, kick Droopy to the curb and let a real man step in.

What's up, star, I like to get to know who you are, let's have drinks at the bar.

Baby, I'm broke, buy me a 40 oz. or something.

Is your father a drug dealer, 'cause you're dope, girl.

Oh honey, with a walk like that, I can see why you have three kids.

Girl, you all that and a bag of chips.

Like Jordan, baby, I got a thirst and you look like my Gatorade.

You look like you can make pretty babies.

If money could buy the body you got, you'd be mine forever.

Hey chicken head, come here.

I'm like Biggie Smalls, I wanna know what your interests are.

Hey baby, we can keep it on the down low.

Please can I give you my pager number, I must get with you.

What's up, Good & Plenty?

Hey, slim goody.

You are my star child.

My crib or yours?

Shorty, could you please hold my hand and dress me?

Your man got nothing to do with me! Give me your number.

Damn, baby, you make my heart go pitty pat.

Hey, dark and lovely.

I like that chocolate chip on your face. Can I take a bite?

Damn, shorty! I didn't know that such big tits come in small packages.

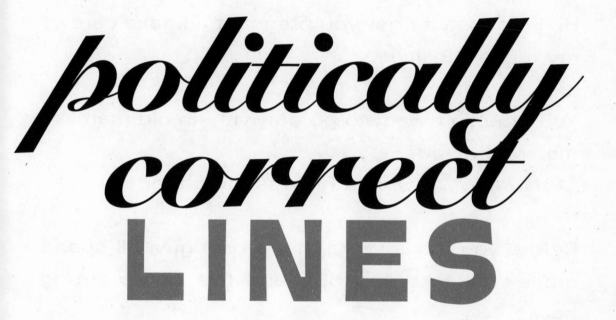

Baby, you know you have to get with me, I have a green card.

Hi, I promise if I get you pregnant, I'll take care of my responsibilities.

You wouldn't want to go out with an old man like me, would you?
Comeback: Only if he was my father.

Before you say a word, I'm a nice guy, I'll spend money, I'll take you out, and I've got a strong back.

Can we be friends, so I can get to know my feminine side?

I live with my baby's mother, but I sleep in another room.

I'm about to get a divorce and I really don't have sex with her anymore.
Comeback: I'm neither a lawyer nor a sex therapist, so I really don't care.

I was married and my wife passed away two years ago. If I gave you my number, would you comfort me?

Sweetheart, you look like a woman who wants a long-term relationship. I have only six months to live, but if you give me your number I know I can live longer.

Oh baby, when I look into your eyes, I see someone I could really care about: me!

I'm the kind of man who deserves to have women I don't deserve.

Yo baby, you are my soul sister and I need some brotherly love.

Girl, I got a Harvard B.A., a Yale J.D., and a German BMW. But I ain't got you.

I don't want your body, I want to get to know your mind.

I'm separated, not married, but we still live in the same house.

If I told you that you have a nice body, would you hold it against me?

I just need a friend to talk to, 'cause my girl is stressing me out and she don't understand me like you do.

I cook, clean, and do windows, all after work.

Do you have to be married to have a baby? 'Cause you and me can have a nice one.

Damn, girl! What you got that makes a black man want to love you so much?

You don't need that guy, 'cause I'll treat you well.

I want to meet your mama to thank her for putting you here on earth.

Baby, I'll give you my home number, 'cause I ain't shacking up with no girlfriend.

116

You look exactly like my second wife, and I married only once.

My mind is telling me no, but my body is telling me yes!

famous
LINES

Do you have any African in you? No. Would you like some?

Oh baby, the bigger the belly, the sweeter the juice.

"You dropped something." "What?" "Our conversation. Let's pick it up from here."

Excuse me, is your husband married?

If I didn't have a girlfriend, I would ask you out. *Comeback:* If I didn't have a boyfriend, I would still say no!

120

Would you like to play chess? Because I would love to be one of your pawns.

You're so fine, you could make a dog like me beg and fetch.

I'm an old-fashioned guy. I would marry you, but I want a lot of practice first.

If I could rearrange the alphabet, I would put U and I together.

What's your sign?
Comeback: I was born under the sign of PMS. You think you're compatible?

121

"Are you married?" "Yes." "Well, I'm not a jealous guy."

If I follow you home, would you keep me?

What's that fragrance you're wearing? It smells so good.
Comeback: It's called Assholes Keep Away.

Do you have a quarter? Because I promised I would call my mother as soon as I fell in love.

Your man must be the luckiest man alive.

Have we worked out in the gym together?

Comeback: No, you're too small.

123

I would do anything for one night of passion with you. *Comeback:* Would you leave?

Come back here, please. Thanks. I just wanted to watch you walk away again.

124

Excuse me, do you have the time?
Comeback: Yes, do you have the energy?

Excuse me, you dropped something—my phone number.

Look, I just called the caterer, now all we have to do is call the church and set a date.

One look at you and I'm speechless.
Comeback: Good, we'll be able to cut all the bullshit.

Excuse me, I didn't catch your name.
Comeback: Sister Catherine.

125

There's something about you that attracts me.
Comeback: Yeah, I went to the doctor about that.

Inheriting 50 million bucks doesn't mean much when you don't have someone to share it with.

Will you marry me?

How you doing? My friend would like to meet you.

You're the most beautiful girl in the world.

Can I take you home?

If I had two hearts, I'd love you with both of them.

Would you like to fall in love with me?

You are the finest thing I've seen all century.

Will you have my baby?

127

Your lips are sweeter than morning dew.

Are you a model?
Comeback: No, I'm a cop.

I know this is corny, but you should be on TV.
Comeback: You're right, it is corny.

Are those your eyes?
Comeback: No, they're glasses.

Haven't I seen you before?
Comeback: Only if you were recently in a line-up.

Didn't we go to school together?
Comeback: I don't think I ever attended reform school.

Is that your girl? No? Then you won't mind if I have her.

You're so good-looking, your wish is my command and I'm ready, willing, and able to be your man.

Are you a doctor? 'Cause I'm lovesick.

You've got a great-looking future behind you.

I never cried in front of a woman before, but when I look at you I could bust out in tears.

I was so struck by your beauty, I had to meet you.

Girl, it must be jam, 'cause jelly don't shake like that.

I've got a taste for something sweet, like a kiss from you.

Where have you been all my life?
Comeback: Kindergarten!

I like your lips. Can I kiss them?

Can I be your friend, your close friend?

Listen, babycakes, you know I'm the one.

It would make my day complete if you would just smile for me.

Excuse me, but could you give me directions to your heart?

I think you're hot!
Comeback: I think you're boring!

Are you Janet Jackson's sister?

I like a woman who knows how to cook. Can you show me?

I'll give you $20 if you remember my name the next time I see you.

Hey baby, let's go to church right now and get married.

133

Hi, is that your baby? She's so pretty, what's your name?

Baby, why you running from the rain? I'll keep you warm.

Is that beauty inherited or did you just get lucky?

Girl, you are the reason I get up in the morning.

You must have a mother named Star, because you sure look like one.

If loving you is wrong, I don't want to be right.

You look like my baby's mother.

Can I take you out sometime? Your boyfriend can join us.

Can I take care of you for the rest of your life?

Excuse me, but aren't you in the movies?

You look like marriage material. What's your name?

135

You're going to fall in love with me, just wait.

Damn, how many boyfriends you got?

I'd love to make you my queen.

I can give you the world, if only you was mine.

Haven't I seen you in my dreams?

I didn't believe in love at first sight until I saw you.

Baby, for a night with you, I'd push up daisies.

Damn, baby, your body is shaped like an hourglass, do you have the time?

unemploy-ment **LINES**

Sweetheart, I'm a little low on cash, but can I put you on layaway?

I'll take you out if you pay for dinner, 'cause I got just enough for the movie.

Excuse me, but I'm short on cash. Could we share the cost of this drink?

Sweetheart, I got no more money for drinks, so either you're going to give me your number or I gotta walk.

How about a date? I got Michael Jordan sneakers and 20 bucks.

140

I would buy you a drink, but I got laid off this morning.

So, what do you do for a living? 'Cause I need a job.

Hi, want another drink? Yes, bartender, she'll have anything under five dollars.

141

Hey baby, I got a token and some Chunkys, you want to go out on a date?

Although I'm not working, I have large assets.

Baby, I'm broke. I'm with Low Budget Productions, Inc. I need a girl with a bank.

Hi, you're cute. Can I borrow 20 bucks?

I would commit robbery if it meant I could steal your love.

Oh! You got your own apartment, too. Can I stay there?

Can I have you now and pay later?

Would you like to go to the movies? I have a great video at home.

I'm not looking for a rich woman, just one who can support me.

Can I give you a ride home? I've got two tokens.

Can I buy you a drink or do you just want money?

Those shoes are fly, can I borrow them?

143

Damn, baby! I know God made tables and chairs just so I could sit next to you.

Baby, when you leave, walk real slow, 'cause I want to know the way to heaven.

Girl, you drop dead born again fine!

Baby, you're so fine, you could make a Baptist go to a brothel.

Mmm! Have mercy on my soul!

You're so fine, you make a Muslim eat pork.

Pinch me. I think I just died and went to heaven.

You smell so good, the Holy Ghost would want to take you to dinner.

Heaven must be missing an angel, because I'm looking right into your eyes.

If you're here, I must have died and gone to heaven.

You look so beautiful, you remind me of the Virgin Mary.

148

Baby, you got it going on. God bless you!

I'm sorry for staring, I've never seen an angel before.

You're so fine, the lord must have dropped you out of the sky.

Baby, you are the complete woman and I wonder if heaven is your true home.

149

Are you an angel in heaven? 'Cause I feel like I'm on cloud nine.

Hey, didn't we meet at the pearly gates of heaven?

Baby, you look so good, you turn saints into sinners.

If I can't have you in this life, can I have you in the next?

Haven't we been together in another life?

When God made you, He damn sure broke the mold.

God bless your mother and father, 'cause having you was a miracle.

Heaven must have sent you from above.

Oh my God! Oh my God! I think I love you.

How was Heaven the last time you were there?

Black goddess that just stepped off the pedestal, allow me to kneel to you in homage to your beauty.

Girl, you're a diamond among the coal, and a quarter among pennies.

Baby, if I could hold you in my arms, I would know what it's like to behold perfection.

Excuse me, miss, there must be a thief some-where, 'cause someone stole the stars from the sky and put them in your eyes.

Girl, what is your secret? Other women get older and you just stay beautiful.

154

Look, I know there are a lot of perfect guys in the world, but I'm one who doesn't watch sports.

You are so beautiful, I swear I see diamonds in your eyes.

Gorgeous, who takes you for walks in the park and buys you ice cream?

I know you don't know me, but would you like to be my friend?

With eyes like that, I would follow you around the world.

If I was Father Time, I would make time stand still, so I could be immersed in your beauty.

You're so fine, you blow my mind and you take my breath away.

All the light
in the sky
can't compete
with the
sunshine you
could bring
into my life.

Girl, your walk, your talk, and the beauty of your smile, all combine in a symphony of loveliness.

Your physical beauty is only surpassed by your exquisite personality.

Oh girl! I know I could never be worthy of your love, but you have my heart at your beck and call.

Baby, I'm yours, do with me as you wish.

Oh girl, happiness would be loving you, and ecstasy would be the tenderness of your warm embrace.

Baby, the touch of your hand and the feeling of your lips on mine would only make my heart want you more.

If you can think of me as much as I am thinking of you, we can make it.

Girl, with you by my side, I would hold the key to success. Without you there is only uncertainty.

Girl, you're so fine, you are my purpose and my way.

You look as beautiful as the sun setting on a waterfall.

I want and need to get to know you.

Gorgeous, I'll treat you like the jewel you are.

I know your man is the happiest man on earth.

I'm a king, let me make you my queen.

With all that gray hair, you must be full of experience.

You're so fine, I know helicopters and planes fall out of the sky for you.

If you listen close enough, you'll hear me calling your name in the wind.

Why don't you smile? I'm sure it will bring the sun out today.

I could tell by your shoes that you have class. I can tell by your purse that you don't have much money.

—Robert Townsend, *Hollywood Shuffle*

Hello, my weakness, how you doin'?

—Damon Wayans, *Mo' Money*

164

Look, girl, if I don't get some trim [sex] before the night's over, I'm gonna bust . . . let's go across the street. By the way, you got any money on you?

—*Eddie Murphy, 48 Hours*

Darling, you're so fine I'll even take out your mother, though she does look like Sonny Liston in a red negligee.

—**Redd Foxx,** *Too Hip for the Room*

You're smart, you're funny, you love life, you're beautiful, you're very sexy, and we have nothing in common.

—*Keenan Ivory Wayans, Low Down Dirty Shame*

165

What if we make love, real hard, for 35 minutes, and then fall into a deep coma-like sleep for 9 hours.

—*Richard Pryor, Harlem Nights*

I wish I had an ice cream, it would look just like you, sweet-tastin' chocolate, good all the way through.

—*Damon Wayans, Mo' Money*

I never accomplished any great feats, but you know what, baby, I'm something else under them sheets.

—*Scatman Crothers, Lady Sings the Blues*

Congress has just ap-
proved me to give you
my heat in a moisture-
seeking MX Missile.

—Spike Lee, *She's Gotta Have It*

I do believe that you and
I were cut out to do
business together.

—Danny Glover, *A Rage In Harlem*

167

You're the best thing that ever happened to me . . . will you marry me?

—Forest Whitaker, *A Rage in Harlem*

168

When I looked at you the first things that came into my mind were cornbread, collard greens, and Wilson Pickett. You got one of those late in the midnight hour bodies.

—*Bill Nunn,* *School Daze*

Were I Pygmalion or God, I would make you exactly as you are in every dimension, from your warm hair to your intimate toes.

—*Glynn Turman,* *Cooley High*

I'm rich, I'm suave, I have a clean navel, I'm full-blooded, I'm a veteran, and you have to get to know me.

—*Bill Cosby,* *A Piece of the Action*

Yo baby, let's go to my place and do the wild thing.

—*Fab 5 Freddy, She's Gotta Have It*

I'll let you do anything you want to me, freaky . . . as long as you don't touch my hair.

—*Eddie Griffin, Jason's Lyric*

Hey girl, tell me where you're going to be, so I can be there, too.

—*Allan Payne, Jason's Lyric*

No one so young as you should be so serious.

—*Angela Bassett, Malcolm X*

I was wondering if maybe we could go out to a movie, restaurant, or pop some Jiffy Pop popcorn together. How about it?

—*Spike Lee, School Daze*

My woman don't understand me like you do, she don't touch me like you do. You the onlyest one I can talk to.

—*Lawrence Fishburne,*
What's Love Got to Do With It

Hey baby, he who hesitates is lost.

—*Sammy Davis Jr., A Man Called Adam*

I've always been attracted to you. I just couldn't tell you before . . . I was shy, but now I'm a different person.

—*Spike Lee, School Daze*

Comeback: Well, I'm not attracted to you.

You look as good as a Spam sandwich on a Ritz cracker.

—*Lawrence Hilton Jacobs*

Sexiness to the left, sexiness to the right, it's all about the pimp sandwich tonight.

—*Morris Day, Graffiti Bridge*

Girl, you're so fine, I would marry your brother just to get into your family.

—Will Smith, *Fresh Prince of Bel Air*

Please baby! Please baby! Baby, baby, baby, please!

—Spike Lee, *She's Gotta Have It*

Girl, you so fine, if I was a hound dog I'd never let you go, 'cause I'd be snapping at you all day and night.

—*Richard Pryor,* *Another You*

If God made anything prettier than you, I hope He kept it for Himself.

—*Will Smith,* *Fresh Prince of Bel Air*

Girl, you so fine, I'd suck your daddy's dick! Is that fine enough for your black ass?

—*Richard Pryor*

Girl, you built to take all my money.

—*Will Smith,* *Fresh Prince of Bel Air*

Here I am all in your Kool-Aid and I don't know your flavor.

—Wesley Snipes, *Waiting to Exhale*

I'm not as good as I once was, but I'm as good once as I ever was!

—Redd Foxx

I see that ring, but I'm just trying to be your friend.

Before you leave, please give me one dance.

I ain't no murderer, baby.

—Lynn Tolliver, WZAK, Cleveland, OH

"Are you married?"
"Yes."
"Do you fool around?"

Hey, I'm not trying to come on to you or anything, but I think that you're one of the prettiest things I've ever seen.

Guys can't take flowers out, but they're pretty and so are you.

—Lena Moore, WWIN, Baltimore, MD
Oh my God, you're beautiful!

"How you doing?"
"Fine."
"You sure are."

If I'm Worf, will you be my Counselor Troi?
Comeback: You watch way too much "Star Trek."

Give me your number or I'll kill myself.

—C.J. Morgan, WQUE, New Orleans, LA

Damn! Monogamy. What a concept.

Baby, I'd walk 20 miles in the snow, backwards, barefoot, across broken glass, just to stand in your garbage and look through your window.

—KC Jones, WVKO, Columbus, OH

Baby, you're so fine I would eat the shit of the dog that pissed on the tires of the laundry truck that takes your dirty drawers to the cleaners.

I'd suck the farts out of your seat covers.

Do you want to screw or do I owe you an apology?

—Carter & Sanborn, WUSL, Philadelphia, PA

I have only six months to live, and I'd like to spend it with you.

I'm gay and I was hoping you could straighten me out.

Your eyes are like limpid pools of eternity.

You remind me of a haunted house; you're mysterious.

—*Juan Conde, WCOX, Richmond, VA*

Are you a **CUD**, cutie on duty?

183

—Mel Marshall, WVAS, Montgomery, AL

Your daddy had to be a bricklayer, because you have such a fine foundation.

(184)

I saw the back of you and that was fine, and now that I see the front, both sides look good.

—*Shauna Sanford, KQXL, Baton Rouge, LA*
I like being with you because I like the way I am when I'm around you.

—*Carol Blackmon, WVEE, Atlanta, GA*
I'll do anything for you . . . if you want coffee, I'll pour it for you.

Have you ever heard of Southern Comfort, because you're looking at it.

Now that we've met, I bet you'll have some good dreams tonight.

—Tami McCall, WQMG, Greensboro, NC
I like a woman with a mustache.

Hey girl, excuse me for noticing, but I like a girl with hairy legs.

You're so fine, I was wondering if I could go on a date with your mother.

Can I have some of your chicken? No, I meant the other piece.

—*Kevin Gardner, WDAS, Philadelphia, PA*

"You got a minute?"
"No."
"Well, you can borrow one of mine."

Now I've seen the two most beautiful things in the world, the Virgin Islands and you.

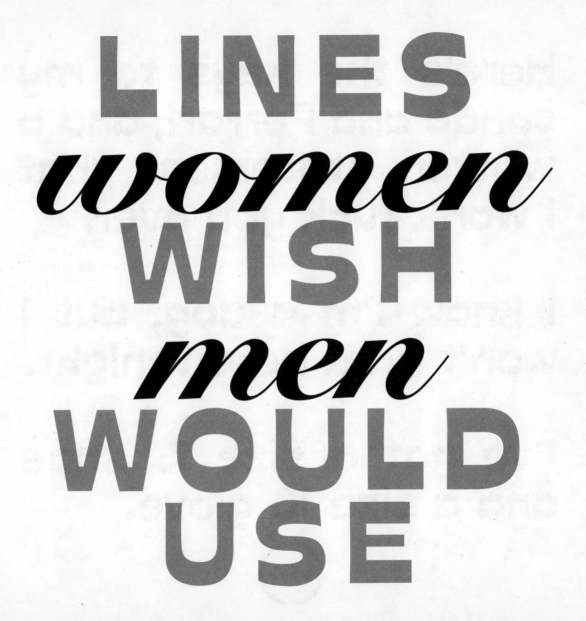

LINES *women* WISH *men* WOULD USE

Here's the keys to my condo and Ferrari, and a written statement that I won't fuck you over.

I know I'm a dog, but I won't bark here tonight.

I've got a size 15 shoe and a size 10 glove.

(190)

I would love to do you without penetration.

I'm a staunch supporter of foreplay.

I have the knowledge and the money, all I need is you.

If you cook the way you walk . . . feed me!

Hi, I'm over 35 with no children, no child support, no drugs, single, heterosexual, I've never been in jail, and I'm available for you.

Hi, I have money and I want to give it to you. I don't care if you're not faithful to me.

I love you, and I'll have the baby.

Excuse me, my Nubian princess, do you have a few minutes of your precious time to spare?

Don't walk yet, let me throw rose petals first so your feet won't travel this polluted world.

I would like to get to know you with no strings attached.

Baby, can I buy you a mink coat?

Hi, I'm looking for a woman in need of a nice house and car.

I believe that women are the superior sex because they can have multiple orgasms.

Can I buy you a drink?

You are the second most beautiful woman in the world, next to my mother.

You've got that million-dollar smile.

Hello sister, how are you feeling?

Sister, you look good today.

I like the way you look, is there any way we can get together?

I believe you are my soulmate.

194

Don't tell me you love me until you get to know me.

I would love to just wake up by your side every morning and cook you breakfast.

I'm cold and I would love to fly you to Hawaii.

Can I be your lumberjack?

195

Baby, just let me take you out to wine and dine you.

God gave the world light just so I could see you.

Hi, here are my test results.

Hello sweetheart, you're a beautiful black sister.

Excuse me queen, can I get a minute of your time?

Hey baby, can I bring you a dozen white roses?

SEE IF YOU CAN FIND YOUR FAVORITE PET NAME:

Pumpkin   Sweetheart   Lovey   Pookey

Slim   Bubba   Shorty   Sugar   Honey   Mookie

Daddy   Big Poppa   Shamu   China   Snooky

Cupcake   Sister Golden Hair   Rhino

Teddy Bear   Sweet & Low   Crown Jewel

200

Baby Cakes   Boo   Sweetness   Sweety Pie
Loverboy   Mister Man   Ms. Thing   Darling
Sugar Bear   Sweething   Twinkle Toes   Candy
Sugar Dumpling   Candy Cane   Ham Hock
Thunder Thighs   Witch Doctor   Toothless Lover
Pork Chop   Bacon Bit   Chuff   My Stuff
Sissy   Custer Pie   Wallo   Woo Woo
My Little Ball Buster   Daddy Long Dick   Rabbit
Hot & Crusty   Boogie   Stud Muffin
Love Machine   Sniffles   Bunion   Sugar Giblets
Pig Feet   Little Love Goddess   Giblet
Little Pork Rind   Sweet Pea   Ganzo   Skully
Blob   Lovebucket   Honey Gizzard   Lord Charles
Candy Man   Biscuit   Scud   Beast
Sexual Chocolate   Jelly Roll   Kingpin

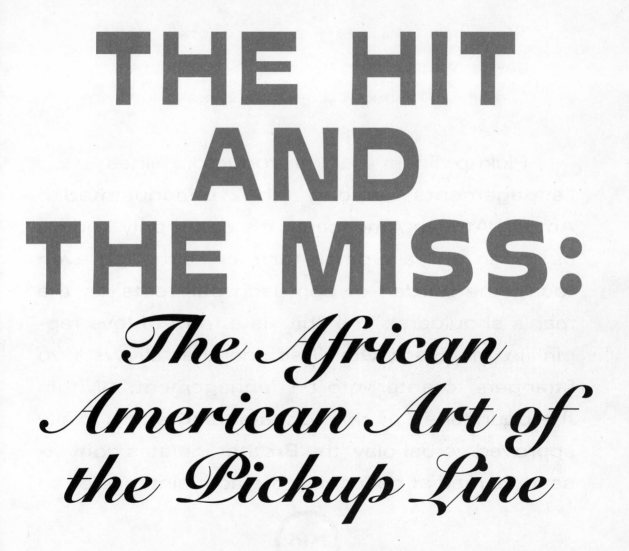

THE HIT AND THE MISS:

The African American Art of the Pickup Line

"You're so fine, I'd marry your brother just to get in your family."

"Baby, all those curves and me with no brakes!"

Pickup lines . . . introductory lines . . . "engagements among the unacquainted."[1] Among African Americans, it's commonly known as "hittin on" a woman (or man, although even today, the burden of approach still rests on the man's shoulders). The "hit" is a form of love rappin' in the Black Oral Tradition that allows two strangers to enter into an "engagement." Within the boundaries of this longstanding and socially approved verbal play, the Brother initiates conversation aimed at deepening the acquaintance of an unknown Sister. The "hittin' on" practice in black courtship grows out of the strongly held belief in the power of Nommo (the Word), a belief so strong that, as Ishmael Reed puts it, "one utters a few words and stones roll aside, the dead are raised and the river beds emptied of their content."[2]

Winning hits are unique expressions of word play, and certain cultural rules govern this verbal tradition. To be successful in winning the woman's ear, the hit must be artfully constructed and expressed with verbal adroitness and flair.

Contrary to popular stereotype, most black men do not regard black women as mere sex objects. Not for one minute—if they are smart—do they underestimate the woman's intellect.

Knowing the Sister's expectations, the Brother invests serious thought and energy in devising engaging, creative, and persuasive lines to introduce into the courtship game. The good hits are a synthesis of emotional and intellectual appeal.

Of course, not all hits, however clever, make a love connection. Hits are a matter of mutual chemistry and timing, and either or both may be off at any given moment. Thus, some hits are constructed to provide the Brother with a safety net, a hedge against rejection, such as "Is your husband married?," to a woman who isn't wearing a wedding ring. The choice is the woman's: "Yes," if she's not interested, "No," if she is. One of the earliest records of this clever attempt at "engagement among the unacquainted" is this 1895 example. "My dear kin miss, has you any objections to me drawing my cher to yer side, and revolvin de wheel of my conversation around the axle of your understandin?"[3]

Playwright Woodie King describes the love rap used by one of his homies during their growing-up days in 1950s Detroit. "Sweet Mac" introduced the Bible into the game to hit on a "foxy, religious" woman:

> I been quoting the Good Book . . . telling her . . . Something or someone is trying to keep us—two pure American religious people of the same order—apart . . . *Thou shalt not covet thy neighbor's wife;* and baby, since you're not any-

body's wife . . . *do unto others as you would have them do unto you* . . . only something like that no-good Satan would want to stop something as mellow as laying naked in the Foggy Night with MJQ or Ravel on the hi-fi . . . He trying to put game on us, momma.[4]

The media often distorts this black verbal art form. The realm of the hit is much deeper than the usual "Hey baby" vernacular lines that have become "ghetto chic" in popular culture these days. In the real world of black male-female relationships, Sisters tend to view the stereotypical phrase with disdain. Several surveys conducted in major metropolitan centers asked black women in all age groups, and across broad socioeconomic lines, to rate greetings used by Brothers in the hittin'-on stage. These opening lines were:

1. Hey, momma!
2. Say, foxy lady!
3. Hi, how you doin?
4. Hey baby, what's happenin?
5. Hello, how are you?

Overwhelmingly, the women preferred (3) and (5). In a more recent study, conducted in a major city in the Midwest, the vernacular, streetified greetings were given a 1990s flavor, and black women, again representing a broad spectrum in age and class, were asked to rate the lines. The results were the same.[5]

This is not to say that bland, everyday lines will get you by, Brothers. But it is to point out that your hit must be something other than those well-worn lines in Hollywood B movies about life in the 'hood, or those lame raps that so quickly get played out on the singles circuit.

Despite the myths about black male super-studs and black hot mommas that continue to persist even as we move into the twenty-first century, surprisingly little research exists on black romance. So we consulted our artistic geniuses, black writers, masters of the word. What follows is a glimpse of portrayals of early courtship in the African American literary tradition.

First, let us say straight up, the Brothers

rarely work in the realm of black romance. It is mainly black women writers who focus on black love and portray our romantic encounters. Most black male writers, past (Langston Hughes, Richard Wright, Ralph Ellison, James Baldwin) and present-day (John Edgar Wideman, David Bradley, Ishmael Reed), tend to be absorbed with the external world—racism, politics, economic injustice. Few focus on the domestic scene. The "real love? Hootchy-gootchy cooing and carrying on?" that Geraldine asks Penny about in John Edgar Wideman's short story "Little Brother"[6] isn't found much in the writing of the Brothers. With black women writers, though, the courtship language and hittin' rhythms of black folks are played out. Initial exchanges range from the play-ful to the supercautious, from the very romantic to the seemingly unemotional encounter.

Take Toni Morrison's Joe and Violet in *Jazz* (1992). They met when he fell out of a black wal-nut tree. Must've been love at first sight for him, 'cause, as he says, "I've been sleeping up there every night. This the first time I fell out."[7] Like the Signifyin' Monkey from "up in the tree,"[8] Joe exchanges clever banter with Violet that underlies the black verbal tradition of signifyin'. When Violet responds, it's on.

"You sleep in trees?"

"If I find me a good one."

"What you doing out here, then, Mr. High and

Mighty, sleeping in trees like a bat?"

"You don't have one nice word for a hurt man?"

"Yeah: find somebody else's tree."

"You act like you own it."

"You act like you do."

"Say we share it."[9]

The uninitiated in the conventions of the black oral tradition might miss the importance of this classic shadow dance between African American men and women. Some personal information is shared, some withheld, boundaries are set, and both Violet and Joe show that they are capable of holding their verbal own with the other. Worthy opponents make worthy companions.

213

In the previous century, African American postslavery texts preached the gospel of "racial uplift" wherein duty to the race was paramount. Frances E. W. Harper's *Iola Leroy* (1892) portrays couples who follow their hearts *and* their duty. As soon as Iola meets the handsome Dr. Latimer, she begins to tell him about her friend Lucy, her "ideal woman—grand, brave, intellectual, and religious." This verbal sparring serves its purpose, providing a subtext that reveals their political bent and also their intense interest in one another. When Dr. Latimer notes that such a woman "would make some man an excellent wife," Iola protests that men always think women are just waiting for a man. Dr. Latimer's response eliminates Lucy from the discussion and hones in on Iola, just as she planned:

> "I think, Miss Leroy, that the world's work, if shared, is better done than when it is per- formed alone. Don't *you* think *your* life-work will be better done if someone shares it with *you?*" asked Dr. Latimer, slowly, and with a smile in his eyes.
>
> "That would depend on the person who shared it," said Iola, faintly blushing.[10]

In later novels, duty comes second to romance. Jody Starks of Zora Neale Hurston's *Their Eyes Were Watching God* (1937) first spies Janie as she is plowing a field. His approach mirrors the easy- going speech of black folk in the 1930s South:

You behind a plow! You ain't got no mo' business wi uh plow than uh hog is got wid uh
holiday! . . . A pretty doll-baby lak you is made
to sit on de front porch and rock and fan yo'-
self and eat p'taters dat other folks plant just
special for you.[11]

Unfortunately, Jody forgot the old adage that what it took to get her is the same thing it takes to keep her. Instead, he confines Janie to a domestic prison in a boring, middle-class, conventional life.

In August Wilson's play, *Fences* (1986), Troy also attracts Rose with a bold line ("I can dance a waltz that'll make you dizzy"),[12] only to lose her through poor follow-through.

Toni Morrison's *Sula* (1973) shows that rap isn't enough unless the brother makes good on his word. Ajax opens Sula's nose, and keeps it open, because he understands the power of follow-through. He doesn't change the style of his approach to Sula as their relationship develops. And his initial one is the approach that opens the door in the first place:

> She opened the heavy door . . . . He smiled and
> said, "I been looking all over for you."
>
> "Why?" she asked.
>
> "To give you these," and he nodded toward one
> of the quarts of milk.
>
> "I don't like milk," she said.
>
> "But you like bottles, don't you?" He held one up.

"Ain't that pretty?"

. . . Laughing, she opened the screen door.[13]

In addition to his "magical" gifts—clusters of black berries, a jar of butterflies he let loose in her bedroom—he respects her mind. "They had genuine conversations. He did not speak down to her or at her . . . He seemed to expect brilliance from her, and she delivered."[14]

Novels are not the only genre in African American letters that bring love lines to the page. Lorraine Hansberry's drama *To Be Young, Gifted and Black* (1969), shows how an industrious Brother can "make a hit" with a topic as mundane as the weather when Candace, a black college student, meets African exchange student Monasse:

218

Candace (laughing and approaching him): If you are that cold, why on earth stand out here?

Monasse: It is cold everywhere in your country. At least, here it is beautiful.

Candace: It is cold everywhere out of doors in my country. We do have steam heat.

Monasse: I am willing to go in if you will have tea with me.

Candace: Tea! Tea, she thought . . . she would try his tea.[15]

Nikki Giovanni's "Kidnap Poem" (1970) takes time out from the militant rhetoric of the civil rights movement to break out into love lines, showing Brothers just how bold Sisters can be:

If I were a poet

I'd kidnap you

put you in my phrases and meter

you to Jones Beach

or maybe Coney Island

or maybe just to my house[16]

Young love, too, is bold—you know it is when his name is Toussaint—in Ntozake Shange's 1977 choreopoem, *for colored girls who have considered suicide when the rainbow is enuf.* Toussaint's opening lines read more like an announcement of himself than a romantic greeting, but they are effective:

'looka heah girl

i am TOUSSAINT JONES

& i'm right heah lookin at ya

& i dont take no stuff from no white folks

ya dont see non round heah do ya? . . .

'come on let's go on down to the docks

& look at the boats' . . .

toussaint jones waz awright wit me.[17]

It goes without saying that physical attraction usually has a lot to do with first approaches. In literature, a character's thoughts might clue us in to the motivation behind his or her first words to a new love interest. Zora, a teacher in Terry McMillan's *Disappearing Acts* (1989), is looking for an apartment when she finds handyman Franklin instead.

"Lord have mercy," was all I heard inside my head.

I couldn't move, let alone speak . . . His eyes looked like black marbles set in almonds . . . His cheeks looked chiseled; his lips succulent. And those shoulders . . . his legs went on forever . . . his arms were the color of black grapes.[18]

Cat-got-your-tongue can put new lovers at a disadvantage. But Franklin runs with Zora's tired rap to show that he's interested in her, too.

"You did a fantastic job on the floors . . . I didn't expect them to turn out this beautiful."

"Thanks . . . I try to do everything good . . . So tell me, are you a Miss or a Mrs.?"

. . . I blurted out, "A Ms . . . Can I ask you a question?"

"Only if it's personal."[19]

As in *Disappearing Acts*, class issues are appearing with more frequency to address the disparity sometimes found between the educational backgrounds and careers of more successful Sisters and their less well-educated suitors. And this class divide can make for some feisty exchanges of love lines. In Bebe Moore Campbell's *Brothers and Sisters* (1994), Tyrone, a delivery man, is at first rebuffed when he tries out his love lines on Esther, a bank manager. But you know the third time's the charm.

"Mr. Carter."

"Call me Tyrone."

"Mr. Carter. If you don't mind, I'm very busy."

223

. . . "I like your style. Can I take you to dinner this Saturday?"

"I'm busy" . . .

"Just got a little chilly up in here." He threw back his head and laughed . . . "All right, Ms. Jackson . . . I'll ask you again."[20]

Tyrone's second attempt is an African-motif invitation that reads

"Please have dinner with me this weekend." It was signed: "Mister Carter." He'd actually spelled out "Mister." Esther chuckled.[21]

Finally captivated, Esther accepts his invitation to "reconnect with [her] culture" by taking in a soul food dinner with him.[22]

The movie version of McMillan's 1992 novel

Waiting to Exhale was stormed by audiences, especially by black women, when it debuted in December 1995. *Exhale* (the book *and* the film) is all about the hits and the misses in the romantic entanglements of four upscale Sisters in Phoenix. Note that as Savannah, the TV executive among the four, circulates at a New Year's Eve party, she responds to the pickup lines as the real-life Sisters respond in the surveys mentioned earlier.

"Yo, Mama, can I follow you?" . . . "How'd you like to bring in the New Year with me, babeeee?" . . . "Sister sister sister. You wearing the hell outta that blue suede dress. Can I take you home with me?" I ignored them . . . I'll be

225

glad when these men learn that if they want to get a grown woman's attention . . . this is not the way to do it . . . I wonder if "Hello, how are you, I'm Carl or Bill or James, and you sure look nice tonight" has ever occurred to them. That's what I want to hear.[23]

What does get her interest is one Brother's ability to manufacture a love line out of a flimsy work connection.

"Hi," he said, in a baritone voice. "Charles Turner, KXIP-TV, San Francisco. How you doing?"

"Savannah Jackson, KPRX-TV, Phoenix. Nice to meet you, Charles."

. . . "Hey," he said. "KPRX is our sister station."[24]

Other scenes in *Exhale* propose that, corny as it may seem, the ol' standbys still work. Michael's opening hit ("Why isn't a beautiful woman such as yourself happily married?") actually flatters Robin, and he clinches it by shrewdly "guessing" her age:

"How old are you?"

"How old do you think I am?"

"Twenty-seven. Twenty-nine at the most."

He got three points for that.[25]

Exhale's James was not only at the right place at the right time; this character, played in the film by superfine Wesley Snipes, also has a way with words. After introducing himself ("My name's James Wheeler. How you doing this evening?"), James attracts the just-divorced Bernadine with this line:

> "You're the most stunning thing I've seen in the four days I've been here."[26]

Gloria is the most down-to-earth of *Exhale*'s four Sisters, and her down-home wisdom decrees simply that the quickest way to a man's heart is through his stomach. Approaching her new neighbor with a fresh-baked sweet potato pie, she combines her culinary skills with not-very-subtle questions to give her the information she wants about his marital status.

> "I'm Gloria Matthews . . . I just wanted to welcome you and your family to the neighborhood."
>
> "Well, thank you . . . . That's sure nice of you.

". . . Come on in for a few minutes."

. . . "Well, I don't want to intrude . . . I just wanted to introduce myself. Is your wife at home?"

"I'm afraid I don't have a wife . . . She passed
away, going on two years now. It's just me here."

"Oh," Gloria said. "I'm sorry to hear that."[27]

Yeah, right. Gloria is so sorry that she promptly
invites him over for dinner to go with that funky
pie she brought over. Not bad. More important,
it worked.

At their best, these love lines are true poetry.
But of course, some poems are better than others. We surely hope that some cogitation on our
elucidation will aid your contemplation and artic-
ulation of sweet salutations to the object of *your*

adoration. And if you don't succeed, please baby, please baby, baby, baby *please* try again.

Geneva Smitherman, Ph.D.

University Distinguished Professor

Department of English

Michigan State University

Gloria Randle, Ph.D.

Assistant Professor

Department of English

Michigan State University

Notes

1. Goffman, Erving. *Behavior In Public Places* (New York: The Free Press,1963), 124.

2. See Smitherman, Geneva. *Talkin and Testifyin: The Language of Black America* (Detroit: Wayne State University Press, 1977), 177.

3. *The Southern Workman* (Hampton University), 1895.

4. King, Woodie. "The Game." *The Black Scholar*, 1965.

5. Smitherman, Geneva. *African American Male-Female Speech Events*. Research In Progress.

6. Wideman, John Edgar. "Little Brother." *Fever: Twelve Stories* (New York: Penguin, 1990), 124.

7. Morrison, Toni. *Jazz* (New York: Plume, 1992), 103.

8. "The Signifying Monkey." *Crossing the Danger Water: Three Hundred Years of African American Writing*, ed. Deirdre Mullane (New York: Doubleday, 1993), 261.

9. *Jazz*, 103–4.

10. Harper, Frances E. W. *Iola Leroy; Or Shadows Uplifted* (Boston: Beacon Press, 1987, 1892), 242–3 (emphasis ours).

11. Hurston, Zora Neale. *Their Eyes Were Watching God* (Urbana: University of Illinois Press, 1978, first published in 1937), 49.

12. Wilson, August. *Fences* (New York: Penguin, 1986), 97.

13. Morrison, Toni. *Sula* (New York; Plume, 1982, first published in 1973), 124.

14. *Sula*, 127–8.

15. Hansberry, Lorraine. *To Be Young, Gifted and Black*. Adapted by Robert Nemiroff (New York: Signet, 1969), 76.

16. Giovanni, Nikki. "Kidnap Poem," *The Women and The Men* (New York: William Morrow and Co., 1975), Part II.

17. Shange, Ntozake. *for colored girls who have considered suicide when the rainbow is enuf* (New York: Collier, 1977), 30.

18. McMillan, Terry. *Disappearing Acts* (New York: Pocket Books, 1989), 24–5.

19. *Disappearing Acts*, 30.

20. Campbell, Bebe Moore. *Brothers and Sisters* (New York: Berkley Books, 1995, first published in 1994), 109-110.

21. *Brothers and Sisters*, 156.

22. *Brothers and Sisters*, 170.

23. McMillan, Terry. *Waiting to Exhale* (New York: Viking Press, 1992), 17.

24. *Waiting to Exhale*, 358–9.

25. *Waiting to Exhale*, 47–8.

26. *Waiting to Exhale*, 283–4.

27. *Waiting to Exhale*, 301–2.

Acknowledg- ments

Thanks to the ladies who hear the lines and were kind enough to share them with us:

Dawn Short, Kelly Ruff, Gloria Stevens, Denise Cater, Geri Sneed, Sherise Hudson, Medea Evans, Susan Duncan, Pam Ponce, Yasmine, Juanne Harris, Tracy Salmon, Lygia Barreto, Betty Faroque, Lisa Ray, Wendy Moten, Cheral Rule, Faith, Yvonne Thomas, Linda Garrett, Thulani Davis, Vivian Taylor, Kelly Campbell, Yolanda Caldwell, Myrna Bootman, Maria Perez,

233

Pasean Wilson, Cheryl Green, Sharon Parker, Margaret Sirot, Carol Green, Robin Exum, Myrna Occasio, Lesonja Webber, Cynthia Averez, Adrianne Lotson, Judith Service, Wanda Holmes, Daphine, Nadja Bellan, Wilma MacDanial, Tina Douglas, Dianne Gibbs, Stephanie Carney, Angela Bunyan, Julie Black, Bridgette Chin, Tracey Archer, Monica Butler, Charmaine Clark, Tyra Taylor, Shay Taylor, Monica Sutton, Nadine Baker, Kellie Jones, Jeanine DuBison, Julie Black, Yvette "Star" Gordon, Valerie Legg, Debbie Pender, Monique Houston, Yvette Coit, Anita Burson, Leah Wilcox, Rhona Greene, Cheryl Abbott, Persina Lucas, Mercedes Ayala, Sharon Alexander, Tye, Nancy Batiste, Rene Gibson, Persis Myers, Pamela Fernandez, Jeanie Davenport, Ronda Fowler,

Sheritty Dey, Valerie Graham, Mugga, Tomeiqua, Donna Baynes, Cooper Cunningham, Jeannie Tate, Gail Goode, Suzanne Vega, Glynace Coleman, Mori MacQueen, Jennifer Mercer, Doreen Whitten, Alyson Williams, Camille O'Garro, Dorothy Chambers, Mary Parker-Harris, Mildred Moore, Vivian Terry, Laura Sanders, Sundra Franklin, Reva Sears, Tuesday Brooks, Diane Mack, Lisa Jeffers

Thanks for the support of these people:

Ian Edwards, T.K. Kirkland, The Comics and Staff of Monty's Comedy Crib, Keith Armstrong, Martine Betancourt & The "Thunder Cats," Ernest Thomas, Bill Branca, Poetic Justice, Dick Scott, Carey Thomas,

Sam Silver, Mike Walton, Louis Bell, Rip It Records, Mike Sargent, Al Dotson, Bob Tate, Roy Smith, Eddie O'Garro, Stanley Winslow, Don Chapman, Guy Rochon, Neil Schwartz, Sean Couch, Bruce Tabb, Fat Joe, Bart Bartolomeo, Imus, Lawrence Hilton Jacobs, Michael Libird, David Gallen, Joe Siegel, Douglas Crew '78, Howard Stern, Ken Webb, Allan Wood, Jeff Redd, Benny Pough, Neil Cogan, Terence Benbow, John Noonan, Myra Hunter, Wendy Christian, House of Ashante, SBC Travel & Tours, Mark & Nicole Graham, Vaughan Dweck, Waverly Ivey

And last, but definitely not least, Mildred Dweck and Ollie Ivey (WE LOVE YOU, MOM).

We would like your comments on this book
as well as any new pickup lines.

I'll Have Two Cheeseburgers and Some Fries, Inc.
P.O. Box 770
New York, New York 10025

or

E-MAIL us at:
Deacon-Blues@msn.com

237

About the Authors

Stephan Dweck and Monteria Ivey are the principals in a New York–based entertainment company I'll Have Two Cheeseburgers and Some Fries, Inc. They have been the subject of articles for the *New York Times,* the *Wall Street Journal,* the *Washington Post,* the *Los Angeles Times,* the *Philadelphia Inquirer,* USA Today, *Vanity Fair,* *Newsweek,* *People* magazine, and *Entertainment Weekly.* They have appeared on the

239

Tom Snyder Show (CNBC), *Charlie Rose* (PBS), CBS News, Fox News, CNN, *Imus in the Morning,* and the *Howard Stern Show.*

Stephan Dweck is a co-author of the best selling books *SNAPS, Double SNAPS,* and *Triple SNAPS.* He is a prominent entertainment attorney specializing in music and television. His clients include over 40 recording artists ranging from current top-40 bands on major labels to underground acts that he cultivates. Stephan also represents over 75 currently-working television and film actors. Stephan sits on the Law Advisory Board for Quinnipiac College School of Law.

240

Monteria Ivey is a comedian/author/actor and the co-author of the best selling books *SNAPS, Double SNAPS,* and *Triple SNAPS.* Monteria was the co-executive producer and host for the HBO *Snaps* television specials. He was the host of *Think Twice,* the first adult game show produced for PBS. Monteria was also the host and a cast member on the *Uptown Comedy Club* syndicated television program. He is affiliated with the Black Filmmaker Foundation, and works regularly for HBO on their stand-up comedy specials as well as the HBO/Toyota Comedy Festival held in New York City.